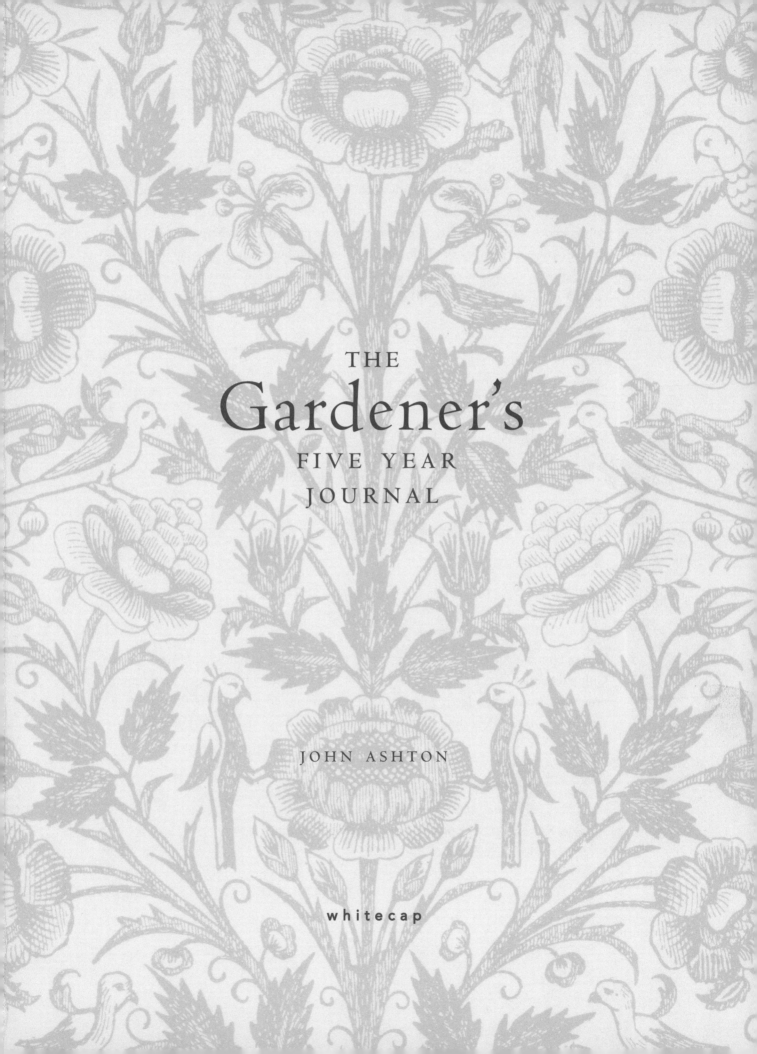

THE
Gardener's
FIVE YEAR
JOURNAL

JOHN ASHTON

whitecap

Edited by Elaine Jones
Cover design by Roberta Batchelor
Interior design by Warren Clark

Printed and bound in Canada

National Library of Canada Cataloguing in Publication Data

Ashton, John, 1944–
 The gardener's five year journal / John Ashton.

 ISBN 1-55285-342-X

 1. Gardening. 2. Diaries (Blank-books) I. Title.
SB450.97.A87 2003   635   C2002-911381-4

The publisher acknowledges the support of the Canada Council for the Arts and the
Cultural Services Branch of the Government of British Columbia for our publishing
program. We acknowledge the financial support of the Government of Canada
through the Book Publishing Industry Development Program for our publishing
activities.

Reproductions of wood engravings (artists unknown): from
A Library of Poetry and Song; edited by Bryant, William Cullen;
Fords, Howard, and Hulbert, New York, 1870.

Introduction

My interest in gardening grew out of genetics and osmosis. I say genetics because each of my parents were avid gardeners in their own right; osmosis, as growing up on an Ottawa Valley farm during the '40s and '50s, the dust and dirt somehow became embedded beneath my fingernails and drifted into my veins. It did not, however, manifest itself to any great degree until well after childhood, which, Father said, was not until I was about twenty-eight!

Very early in our marriage, Janet and I, with boundless energy and enthusiastic optimism, planted our first vegetable garden. I thought that my farming genes, along with the will to toil, would give me the intrinsic ability to produce a garden equivalent to that of my parents. It soon became painfully clear that love and labor were not enough. My primitive knowledge of soil requirements, seeding techniques and plant care yielded a crop that could only be described as pitiful. My childhood memories of working in the garden had not served me well (my folks always questioned how I could remember something I never actually did) but, through reading, observing, talking with experts and using my tricky "by-guess-and-by-God" method, I can now declare a modicum of success.

My father said that if you can't be smart at least be organized, so I got organized! Unfortunately, I didn't do it soon enough, and I now regret that. Had I been organized enough to keep records of my gardening attempts, I would still have the name of those tomato plants that yielded fruit the size of softballs, and I'd be able to find out the variety of peppers that produced enough fruit to completely fill three large plastic garbage bags. I also wish I could remember the name of the pencil beans I planted sometime in the mid '70s, as I do not want them again: they had the consistency and taste of old boot leather! But I finally clued in to the fact that gardening really starts the year—or even several years—before one starts to actually garden. (Those of you who grow asparagus will know what I mean.) Now I am both smart *and* organized, and I simply turn back the pages to find those elusive variety names.

This journal is meant to help prevent the loss of important names, dates and gardening efforts that will surely become blurred over time. (Don't delude yourself about this—I did, but I didn't get away with it!) Although I have included a few tips and techniques (mostly for beginners, as I do not wish to insult the intelligence of seasoned gardeners), this journal is *not* a source of gardening techniques, but rather an easy-to-use workbook that allows and encourages gardeners to record their own particular activities.

Contents

Acknowledgments

I wish to express my sincere appreciation to my friends and fellow gardening enthusiasts for their advice and encouragement: Katie and John Dawson, Bernadette Greene, Joanne and Ron Guille, and Helen and Jim Lang. Without their suggestions this journal would not be as widely inclusive as it is. Thank you, all.

A special thank you to my own family: my son, Scott, for his many suggestions and countless hours on the computer; my daughter, Heather, for her editorial advice; and my dear wife, Janet, my most ardent adviser and supporter. For the text on collecting and saving seeds, many thanks to my brother, Doug Ashton, a seed biologist with the Canadian Food Inspection Agency.

My final word of thanks goes to the staff of Whitecap Books: Leanne McDonald, rights and acquisitions associate, who was largely instrumental in securing Whitecap's acceptance of my initial idea and who guided me through the world of publishing; Robin Rivers, editorial director, who artfully directed the journal to its final conclusion; and, finally, editor Elaine Jones, who polished the final text.

To the memory of my parents,
Lois & Percy Ashton

The kiss of the sun for pardon,
The song of the birds for mirth,
One is nearer God's heart in a garden
Than anywhere else on earth.

—Dorothy Gurney

To inspire young, budding gardeners, the journal includes five pages, one for each year, for children.

Watching children plant, care for and harvest their own produce is a rewarding experience, and one that can turn your gardening projects into family events. Children can keep their own simple records, map the location of their plants, take photos and compare their results with last year.

Before the next growing season, and while you are reviewing your new seed catalogues, look back in your journal to find the varieties and techniques that worked best for you. Review notes you made in "Plans and Recommendations" during past years, and plan with the comfort and knowledge that you have done all you can to ensure even more fruitful results.

Here's to healthier plants, larger yields, greener greens and, of course, a better memory.

John Ashton
North Saanich, British Columbia
June 2002

*All gardeners need to know when to accept
something wonderful and unexpected, taking no
credit except for letting it be.*

—Clara Balfour

Night

How beautiful this night! the balmiest sigh
Which vernal zephyrs breathe in evening's ear
Were discord to the speaking quietude
That wraps this moveless scene.

—Percy Bysshe Shelley

PLANNING THE GARDEN

Garden Layout

The pages in this section will give you a five-year record of where the plants in your garden are located—whether it be a vegetable garden, cutting garden or a mixed garden bed. Using the dots as row markers, locate each variety grown.

For those with vegetable gardens, the importance of crop rotation (see page 26) cannot be over-emphasized, and careful record-keeping will ensure that crops are not planted in the same place in succeeding years. Simply refer back to the previous year's diagram to determine the new location of your plantings. Even though the seeding and transplanting charts will give a record of the seeds purchased for any particular year, it might prove worthwhile to add descriptive details about each variety on these pages. An example might be: "Corn – Aladdin – Extra Early Bicolour – 60 days – planted May 20." Those who have raised beds rather than large garden plots will also find the crop rotation section useful for keeping track of plantings.

I'm a careless potato, and care not a pin
How into existence I came;
If they planted me drill-wise, or dibbled me in,
To me 'tis exactly the same.
The bean and the pea may more loftily flower,
But I care not a button for them;
Defiance I nod with my beautiful flower,
When the earth is hoed up to my stem.

—Thomas Moore

Garden Layout

Year:

Scale:

Garden Layout

Year:

Scale:

Garden Layout

Year:

Scale:

Garden Layout

Year:

Scale:

Garden Layout

Year:

Scale:

Property Plan

The following six grids will help you plan landscape changes to your property over the next five years. For example, on the first grid, draw a master plan of your property showing all significant characteristics—trees, outbuildings, ponds, gardens, house location, driveway, hedges, etc. Each year for the next five years, use a new grid to plan changes you wish to make, be they major or minor. It will be interesting to compare your original landscape with that of year five.

To facilitate planning, you might wish to purchase a piece of clear acetate and a few colored, non-permanent markers. Position the acetate over your master plan and use the markers to draw in new ideas for pathways, rock gardens, plantings or any other changes you have in mind. Your ideas and designs may take several tries, but that is the whole point of the overlay —to rework your plans as often as required. After you have completed the outdoor projects, make the changes on the paper grid, giving you a permanent record of what you have accomplished for the year. The overlay can then be cleaned off and readied for your next set of ideas.

Another way to use these grids is to allocate each grid to a particular area of your property, drawing in, labelling, and noting the date of completion for the changes made to each area.

So plant your own garden
and decorate your own soul,
instead of waiting for someone
to bring you flowers

—Author unknown

Property Plan

Scale:

Year:

Property Plan

Year:

Scale:

Year:

Scale:

Property Plan

Year:

Scale:

Property Plan

Scale:

Year:

Property Plan

Scale:

Year:

Soil Tests

The ultimate dream of every gardener is to work in loam, otherwise known as "black gold." This is a combination of clay, sand and humus (decayed organic matter) mixed in proper proportions. Unfortunately, loam never seems to be where I actually require it; whenever I lift sod for a new garden, all I ever seem to find is either clay or sand, but never loam. I suspect there are countless would-be gardeners who, upon discovering the complete absence of loam in their newly dug plot, quickly abandon all thoughts of gardening, replace the sod, and leave the production of vegetables to their local grocery store. Do not despair; although it will take time to achieve the correct potent consistency, you can manufacture your own "black gold" with approximately one-third clay, one-third sand, and one-third humus.

For determining the correct balance of nitrogen, phosphorus and potash (N, P, K), I find soil-testing kits to be accurate, rapid and very easy to use. You can get these kits at nurseries. I strongly recommend testing your soil after the fall harvest and especially when starting a new garden. This is a good time to balance the soil or replace elements that have become depleted. Soil amendments require time to combine with soil organisms in order to make them readily available for spring planting. Once you have established a nutrient-rich soil, a yearly feeding of mulches and compost should maintain soil balance. However, it's worth testing your soil on a regular basis to make sure it remains healthy.

Included in this section is a chart for recording soil formulas for plants that require special recipes. For instance, 2 parts loam + 1 part peat moss + 1 part washed sand + 1/4 part dried manure = a good general recipe for house or bench plants. Other gardening formulas that could also be recorded here are those household recipes using common ingredients found around the house. Our neighbor recently provided us with the following green-up tonic: 1 can beer + 1 cup ammonia + 1/2 cup baby shampoo + 1/2 cup liquid lawn food + 1/2 cup molasses or corn syrup, all mixed in a 20 gallon sprayer of warm water. There are many commercially prepared soils and tonics available but you may wish to try your own formulas, in which case this chart will be an invaluable tool for recording the ingredients and results of your experiments.

To dig and delve in nice clean dirt
Can do a mortal little hurt.

—John Kendrick Bangs

Soil Tests

Date	Soil Location	pH	Nitrogen	Phosphorous	Potash	Action Taken

Soil Formulas and Garden Recipes

Plant	Formula	Result	Source

Crop Rotation

Crop rotation increases both the quality and quantity of vegetable crops and should be practiced on a yearly basis. Exceptions are asparagus, rhubarb and Jerusalem artichoke, which are planted in permanent beds.

Moving crops from one area to another can significantly decrease the changes of a buildup of diseases and insects that affect specific families of vegetables. Another advantage of rotation is avoiding nutrient depletion. Legumes, for instance, fix nitrogen in the soil, making it available for the next crop, so legume crops can be followed with heavy nitrogen feeders such as brassicas.

Fortunately, we can use a simplified system that assigns vegetables to four groups: brassicas, root and solanaceous vegetables, legumes and alliums.

- Brassicas include broccoli, Brussels sprouts, cabbage, cauliflower, kale, kohlrabi, turnip, radish, bok choi.
- Solanaceous and root crops include sweet peppers, tomatoes, eggplants, celery, beets, carrots, sweet potatoes, potatoes, parsnips.
- Legumes include beans, peas, okra.
- Alliums include onions, scallions, leeks, garlic.

Cucumber and squash (both in the cucurbit family) and corn do not fit into these major groups, but can be added to one or more of them—alliums, for example—and rotated accordingly.

Here is an example of how the various groupings could be rotated.

	Year 1	Year 2	Year 3	Year 4	Year 5
Bed 1	Legumes	Brassicas	Alliums	Root Crops	Repeat Year 1
Bed 2	Root Crops	Legumes	Brassicas	Alliums	
Bed 3	Alliums	Root Crops	Legumes	Brassicas	
Bed 4	Brassicas	Alliums	Root Crops	Legumes	

The charts that follow are suited to raised beds, or small plots. By filling in a particular month with the cultivars you planted, it will be easy to avoid planting the same crop in the same bed the following years. I have included the winter months as those of us lucky enough to live on the west coast can take advantage of the many plants that thrive in a temperate climate.

Crop Rotation

Year	January February	March April	May June	July August	September October	November December
Bed 1						
Bed 2						
Bed 3						
Bed 4						

Year	January February	March April	May June	July August	September October	November December
Bed 1						
Bed 2						
Bed 3						
Bed 4						

Crop Rotation

Year	January February	March April	May June	July August	September October	November December
Bed 1						
Bed 2						
Bed 3						
Bed 4						

Crop Rotation

Year	January February	March April	May June	July August	September October	November December
Bed 1						
Bed 2						
Bed 3						
Bed 4						

Crop Rotation

Year	January February	March April	May June	July August	September October	November December
Bed 1						
Bed 2						
Bed 3						
Bed 4						

Contentment

Turn, Fortune, turn thy wheel with smile or frown;
With that wild wheel we go not up or down;
Our hoard is little but our hearts are great.

—Joshua Sylvester

Planting

Seeding & Transplanting

Before I started to keep records, I would try to remember (without much success) which seeds I had grown the previous year, when they were started, where they were purchased and their cost. A permanent record now allows me to refer back to such data, eliminating the cost of duplication and allowing me to plan for seeding and transplanting.

Most seeds can be stored in a cool, dry area for three to five years. (An exception is parsnip, which rapidly loses its ability to germinate after a year.) To determine if your leftover seeds are still viable, sprinkle a few of them between wet paper towels. If most of them do not sprout within seven to ten days, it is better to toss them out and start over.

The "Amount to Re-order" column in the following chart will save you the tedious task of having to empty those fifteen coffee cans, each stuffed with old seed packets, trying to discover what to order for the upcoming season. It is also interesting to compare the price of the same variety from year to year.

The majority of gardeners have not taken gardening courses. Most of us gained our knowledge from our own experimenting, reading gardening books and articles, asking a knowledgeable neighbor or joining a local gardening club. Gardening, like most everything else, allows for certain procedures to be carried out in a multitude of ways, each leading to its own level of success.

You know as well as I do that no matter what tips I might suggest, there will always be those who vehemently say, "That's not the way Grandma and Grandad used to do it!" Therefore, I leave it up to you, the reader, to choose and develop your own methods of seeding and transplanting. I will put forward only one strong suggestion for the beginning gardener, and it is this: follow the directions on the seed packages. The seed companies are the experts (they have a strong interest in your success with their seeds, after all!), and their advice should be well-heeded. Planting depth, germination temperature, transplanting time, distance apart and soil requirements are some of the recommendations normally found on packaged seeds.

If seeds in the black earth can turn into such beautiful roses, what might not the heart of man become in its long journey towards the stars.

—G.K. Chesterton

Seeding and Transplanting

YEAR

Type	Variety	Start Seed Indoors	Transplant to Garden	Direct Seed to Garden	Germination	Source	Price	Amount to Re-order
							TOTAL	

Seeding and Transplanting

YEAR

Type	Variety	Start Seed Indoors	Transplant to Garden	Direct Seed to Garden	Germination	Source	Price	Amount to Re-order
								TOTAL

Seeding and Transplanting

YEAR

Type	Variety	Start Seed Indoors	Transplant to Garden	Direct Seed to Garden	Germination	Source	Price	Amount to Re-order
							TOTAL	

Seeding and Transplanting

YEAR

Type	Variety	Start Seed Indoors	Transplant to Garden	Direct Seed to Garden	Germination	Source	Price	Amount to Re-order
								TOTAL

Seeding and Transplanting

YEAR

Type	Variety	Start Seed Indoors	Transplant to Garden	Direct Seed to Garden	Germination	Source	Price	Amount to Re-order
								TOTAL

Plant Requirements

There are now pills we can take to improve memory, and I must admit to having tried them. Unfortunately, I kept forgetting to take them, so eventually I just gave up. When it comes to my precious garden I hate to forget anything (I strongly suspect that someday I will forget that I even have a garden!), but there is so much information about plant requirements that it has become necessary to keep records. This is particularly true in springtime, when planting is in full swing.

Rather than leafing through a multitude of sources, I can now go directly to my records to determine the requirements of each vegetable, flower, shrub, vine, berry and tree. It is also useful in the fall when I am preparing the beds for the next growing season. This chart allows for the recording of specific requirements—pH, fertilizer, light, soil and water needs—for your most important plants. Use the "Comments" space to record bits of information gleaned from various sources.

Plant	pH	Fertilizer requirements	Sun, shade, partial	Soil type	Water needs
Asparagus	7.5	Slow release 16-4-4	Full Sun	Manure-rich Well-drained Sandy loam	Lots of water

Comments—plant tomatoes nearby to discourage asparagus beetles—add seaweed to bed in fall—keep soil slightly alkaline (add lime in fall)—keep well weeded—cut spears at an angle below surface—parsley planted near asparagus compliments growth of each

You can't forget a garden
When you have planted seed—
When you have watched the weather
And know a rose's need!

—Louise Driscoll

Plant Requirements

Plant	pH	Fertilizer requirements	Sun, shade, partial	Soil type	Water needs	Comments
Plant	pH	Fertilizer requirements	Sun, shade, partial	Soil type	Water needs	Comments
Plant	pH	Fertilizer requirements	Sun, shade, partial	Soil type	Water needs	Comments
Plant	pH	Fertilizer requirements	Sun, shade, partial	Soil type	Water needs	Comments
Plant	pH	Fertilizer requirements	Sun, shade, partial	Soil type	Water needs	Comments
Plant	pH	Fertilizer requirements	Sun, shade, partial	Soil type	Water needs	Comments
Plant	pH	Fertilizer requirements	Sun, shade, partial	Soil type	Water needs	Comments
Plant	pH	Fertilizer requirements	Sun, shade, partial	Soil type	Water needs	Comments

Plant Requirements

Plant	pH	Fertilizer requirements	Sun, shade, partial	Soil type	Water needs	Comments
Plant	pH	Fertilizer requirements	Sun, shade, partial	Soil type	Water needs	Comments
Plant	pH	Fertilizer requirements	Sun, shade, partial	Soil type	Water needs	Comments
Plant	pH	Fertilizer requirements	Sun, shade, partial	Soil type	Water needs	Comments
Plant	pH	Fertilizer requirements	Sun, shade, partial	Soil type	Water needs	Comments
Plant	pH	Fertilizer requirements	Sun, shade, partial	Soil type	Water needs	Comments
Plant	pH	Fertilizer requirements	Sun, shade, partial	Soil type	Water needs	Comments

Plant Requirements

Plant	pH	Fertilizer requirements	Sun, shade, partial	Soil type	Water needs	Comments
Plant		Fertilizer requirements	Sun, shade, partial	Soil type	Water needs	Comments
Plant		Fertilizer requirements	Sun, shade, partial	Soil type	Water needs	Comments
Plant		Fertilizer requirements	Sun, shade, partial	Soil type	Water needs	Comments
Plant		Fertilizer requirements	Sun, shade, partial	Soil type	Water needs	Comments
Plant		Fertilizer requirements	Sun, shade, partial	Soil type	Water needs	Comments
Plant		Fertilizer requirements	Sun, shade, partial	Soil type	Water needs	Comments
Plant		Fertilizer requirements	Sun, shade, partial	Soil type	Water needs	Comments

Plant Requirements

Plant	pH	Fertilizer requirements	Sun, shade, partial	Soil type	Water needs	Comments
Plant	pH	Fertilizer requirements	Sun, shade, partial	Soil type	Water needs	Comments
Plant	pH	Fertilizer requirements	Sun, shade, partial	Soil type	Water needs	Comments
Plant	pH	Fertilizer requirements	Sun, shade, partial	Soil type	Water needs	Comments
Plant	pH	Fertilizer requirements	Sun, shade, partial	Soil type	Water needs	Comments
Plant	pH	Fertilizer requirements	Sun, shade, partial	Soil type	Water needs	Comments
Plant	pH	Fertilizer requirements	Sun, shade, partial	Soil type	Water needs	Comments

Collecting Seeds

By the time I was in grade one I was allowed to miss a few days of school during planting season, as my father needed me on the back of the seeder to help with the distribution of seed. Even at this early stage of my educational career, I had already concluded that sitting at a desk was not a whole lot of fun. I took great pride in being allowed to help my father with such an important task, and this, coupled with the sheer delight of missing school, gave me a very positive early association with seeds.

Never having been a student of the sciences, I would much rather plant seeds than study them. Except for collecting, saving and replanting a few marigold and zinnia seeds, my expertise in the field of plant propagation is rather limited. As luck would have it, my brother, Doug, is a seed biologist with the Canadian Food Inspection Agency. Doug, with his vast knowledge of seeds, immediately sprang to mind when my publisher asked that I include a section on collecting and saving seeds. I am delighted and proud to present Doug's response.

If you want to collect seed and save it for planting at a later date, you should keep this in mind during the growing season. Look for robust plants having the characteristics you want to reproduce, and mark them with a loosely tied piece of colored ribbon or yarn.

To avoid the disappointment of watching your carefully selected seed develop into a plant with none of the characteristics you were looking for, don't collect seeds from plants that are not themselves sold in seed form. Seeds from vegetatively propagated plants such as fruit trees, berries, potatoes, plants from bulbs and many ornamentals, as well as seed from hybrids, will not produce plants that resemble the variety.

In most cases, the seeds must reach maturity while still attached to the mother plant, which requires that the plant be left in the garden until it has dried and turned brown. Mature seed will be dry and easily separated from the mother plant.

The harvesting method you use will depend on the nature of the "container" holding the seeds on the plants. If the mature seeds are held in dry heads, pods or capsules, it is simply a matter of mechanically breaking the structures apart to release the seeds. Some plants will naturally "shatter" and seeds may be lost. To avoid this, cut the plants when the seeds begin to ripen and lay them on a cloth onto which the early seeds will fall. Later, seeds can be threshed out. Threshing can be accomplished by any means that will break apart the enclosing structure, such as rubbing between your hands, gentle flailing or rolling with a rolling pin with light pressure. Remember that when seeds are dry they may be quite brittle and can be damaged in the threshing process.

Seeds enclosed in fleshy fruits such as tomato or melon require a different harvesting method. Select fully ripe fruit, cut them, and squeeze or scoop out the pulp and seeds into a pan or bucket. Let the pulp, seeds and juice sit at room temperature for a few days, stirring occasionally. The pulp will ferment and break down and the seeds will drop to the bottom of the liquid. Warmer temperatures will speed the fermentation process. Once it appears that most of the seeds have been released, add water, stir, let the seeds settle, and pour off the liquid. Repeat the rinsing until the seeds are clean. Lay the seeds out in a thin layer on a fine screen or cloth for one or two days to dry.

Once the seeds are threshed or extracted, you will probably need to clean away some debris. A gentle breeze from a fan can help blow off the chaff and some of the poorer, under-filled seeds. For best results hand-pick the seeds, selecting the plumpest and healthiest.

While stories of 2,000-year-old viable seeds being recovered from ancient Egyptian tombs are not true, it is true that under favorable conditions seeds can survive for many years. Success at saving seed depends heavily on three factors—seed moisture content, temperature and humidity. The seed you have collected should be very dry. If you suspect the moisture content to be too high, lay them out to air-dry for a few days on a cloth or fine screen,

in a warm, dry area. Seeds extracted from fleshy fruits may be laid out in the sun to dry, but otherwise, seeds should not be placed in direct sunlight as the heat could damage them. The greatest enemy of seed viability is the combination of high temperatures and high humidity. Seed will survive quite well for one to three years at room temperature, provided the relative humidity is below 65%. In cold climates the humidity indoors is much lower than this, so overwintering at room temperature is quite safe. The seeds can be stored in paper envelopes or cloth bags. Sealable glass jars can also be used and may extend the viability of the seed for several years, particularly if kept in a cool place. The other enemies of seed are fungi, insects and rodents. Fungi should not be a problem if the seed is properly dried and stored in an area of low humidity. If after storage your seed smells musty, fungi have been at work and viability may have been jeopardized. When storing, make sure there aren't any insects in the seed, and select a site that will keep out insects and rodents.

A final word of caution: If your objective is to sell or otherwise distribute your seed, you should first verify that the variety is not protected under plant breeders' rights laws.

—Doug Ashton

Accuse not nature;
She has done her part
Do thou but thine.

—John Milton

Collecting Seeds

Plant Name	Date Collected	Storage Method	Date Planted	Germination Success

Collecting Seeds

Plant Name	Date Collected	Storage Method	Date Planted	Germination Success

Plant Propagation

The term *plant propagation* refers to the multitude of methods used to start new plants. Plants are reproduced sexually (seed) and vegetatively (cuttings, division, grafting, and layering). Vegetative methods ensure that the resulting plants will be identical to the parent plant.

If you have patience and are willing to do the work, vegetative propagation can be most satisfying and rewarding for both increasing your own garden stock and providing new stock for family and friends. Perennials can be divided, fruit trees grafted, roses layered and new plants can be produced from hardwood and softwood cuttings. The topic of vegetative propagation is as detailed as it is varied, and well beyond the mandate of this journal. You can learn the techniques and procedures from local experts and/or the many books that discuss propagation in detail.

God Almighty first planted a Garden. And indeed it is the purest human pleasure.
It is the greatest refreshment to the spirits of man; without which buildings and
palaces are but gross handy works and a man shall ever see that when ages grow
to civility and elegancy, men come to build stately sooner than to garden finely;
as if gardening were the greater perfection.

—Francis Bacon "Of Gardens"

Plant Propagation

Plant Name	Technique Used	Success Rate	New Location/Destination

Plant Propagation

Plant Name	Technique Used	Success Rate	New Location/Destination

The Daisy Wreath

Sweet Daisy! oft I talk to thee,
Thou unassuming common-place
Of nature, with that homely face,
And yet with something of a grace
Which love makes for thee!

—William Wordsworth

PLANT CARE

Keeping a Maintenance Record

During the winter, Father would hitch up his faithful team of Molly and Prince to the manure sled, fork it full of steaming, pungent manure, and head into the fields. There, in preparation for spring, he'd pitch-fork his "barn-grown" fertilizer over the snow-covered ground. The previous fall, a more aged manure had been forked onto the vegetable patch after harvesting, first-hand experience telling him that fresh manure on spring-planted vegetables can, in many cases, do more harm than good. Beside his mound of mulching straw, he had several "variety" piles of cow, horse, pig and chicken manure, all outrageously odorous and each slotted for a particular field or crop. If you have ever forked year-old manure from a chicken house in early spring, you will know that it is not one of life's sweet pleasantries. It was one of my chores, and Mother made sure I undressed in the stoop before allowing me to re-enter her kitchen—or any place else for that matter!

Today, for those of us who toil in our suburban gardens, these old-fashioned manure piles can be avoided. Many nurseries and garden outlets do provide great piles of the stuff, but they have probably been drained, churned, puréed and cured so they have a more acceptable aroma. And for every berry, flower, vegetable, shrub and tree, whether healthy or diseased, whether grown in muck, clay, sand or loam, there seem to be umpteen commercial fertilizers, each with a specific duty to perform. Libraries, bookstores and most garden centers have countless resources on fertilizing, mulching, spraying and pruning. I would strongly urge both budding and ripened gardeners to educate themselves (or re-educate, as the case may be) about the many options and products available.

For the beginner, one word of caution: if you opt for commercial fertilizers and sprays, diligently follow the manufacturer's instructions and recommendations. Trying to triple your tomato crop by tripling your fertilizing program...well, it just won't work! As well, indiscriminate spraying of every living insect that sets foot in your garden is not a good idea; there are many beneficial insects that contribute to good garden health, such as ladybugs. Many garden centers now provide a wide array of these beneficial predators as an alternative to harmful pesticides. Similarly, many plant diseases can be controlled with the use of less harmful remedies, examples of which may be found on the Internet, at the library, or at your friendly local garden center.

After consulting your local sources to establish the best fertilizing dates of particular plants in your area, take the time to fill in the "Recommended Dates" column. Once completed, you won't have to do it again for another five years when, hopefully, you will purchase another *Gardener's Five Year Journal.* The chart will allow you to compare your actual completion date with the recommended date over a five-year period. Close examination of these dates may reveal a pattern that might allow you to forecast weather cycles, determine earlier or later than normal planting influences or the prediction of crop yields. You may even end up as the gardening guru of the neighborhood!

What a man needs in gardening is
a cast-iron back with a hinge in it.

—Charles Dudley Warner

Fertilizing & Mulching

For recommended dates in your area, consult your local gardening sources. Always follow manufacturer's product recommendation.

Recommended Dates	Plant/Area Treated	Product Used	Year____ Date Done	Year____ Date Done	Year____ Date Done	Year____ Date Done	Year____ Date Done	Year____ Date Done

Fertilizing & Mulching

For recommended dates in your area, consult your local gardening sources. Always follow manufacturer's product recommendation.

Recommended Dates	Plant/Area Treated	Product Used	Year ___ Date Done	Year ___ Date Done	Year ___ Date Done	Year ___ Date Done	Year ___ Date Done	Year ___ Date Done

Plant Name	Problem	Treatment Date	Treatment	Result

Plant Name	Problem	Treatment Date	Treatment	Result

Pruning

For recommended dates in your area, consult your local gardening sources.

Recommended Dates	Plant Name	Comments	Year____ Date Done	Year____ Date Done	Year____ Date Done	Year____ Date Done	Year____ Date Done

Pruning

For recommended dates in your area, consult your local gardening sources.

Recommended Dates	Plant Name	Comments	Year___ Date Done	Year___ Date Done	Year___ Date Done	Year___ Date Done

Honest Toil

These are the hands whose sturdy labour brings
The peasant's food, the golden pomp of kings.

—Oliver Wendell Holmes

PLANT INVENTORY

Keeping a Plant Inventory

The barn I once played and worked in (my folks would probably question the word "worked," but honestly, I do remember milking cows, shovelling manure, and pitching hay!) remains standing today, and it was only a few years ago that I delighted in exploring it once again. Just inside the main door were a few whitewashed old boards supported by wonky legs, which my father used as a writing surface. On it he kept a tattered scribbler in which he would record his daily milk and egg production and other inventories of rural concerns, such as grain production, spring seed requirements, crop rotations, costs of machine repairs and so on. I like to think my inclination for record keeping has something to do with my father's simple desk in that rather tranquil setting fifty years ago.

Consider passing down your journal to a family member. I only wish my father had kept his scribbler, not only for sentimental reasons, but also because it might have contained some interesting tips and ideas that I could apply to my own garden today.

My heart shall be thy garden.
Come, my own into thy garden;
Thine be happy hours
Amongst my fairest thoughts,
My tallest flowers,
From root to crowning petal thine alone.

—Alice Megnell

Annuals

Variety	Description	Date Planted	Location	Number Planted	Special Characteristics	Supplier

Variety	Description	Date Planted	Location	Number Planted	Special Characteristics	Supplier

Annuals

Variety	Description	Date Planted	Location	Number Planted	Special Characteristics	Supplier

Annuals

Variety	Description	Date Planted	Location	Number Planted	Special Characteristics	Supplier

Berry Bushes

Variety	Description	Date Planted	Location	Number Planted	Special Characteristics	Supplier

Bulbs

Variety	Description	Date Planted	Location	Number Planted	Special Characteristics	Supplier

Bulbs

Variety	Description	Date Planted	Location	Number Planted	Special Characteristics	Supplier

Fruit Trees

Variety	Description	Date Planted	Location	Number Planted	Special Characteristics	Supplier

Fruit Trees

Variety	Description	Date Planted	Location	Number Planted	Special Characteristics	Supplier

Perennials

Variety	Description	Date Planted	Location	Number Planted	Special Characteristics	Supplier

Perennials

Variety	Description	Date Planted	Location	Number Planted	Special Characteristics	Supplier

Perennials

Variety	Description	Date Planted	Location	Number Planted	Special Characteristics	Supplier

Perennials

Variety	Description	Date Planted	Location	Number Planted	Special Characteristics	Supplier

Perennials

Variety	Description	Date Planted	Location	Number Planted	Special Characteristics	Supplier

Roses

Variety	Description	Date Planted	Location	Number Planted	Special Characteristics	Supplier

Roses

Variety	Description	Date Planted	Location	Number Planted	Special Characteristics	Supplier

Shrubs & Vines

Variety	Description	Date Planted	Location	Number Planted	Special Characteristics	Supplier

Shrubs & Vines

Variety	Description	Date Planted	Location	Number Planted	Special Characteristics	Supplier

Shrubs & Vines

Variety	Description	Date Planted	Location	Number Planted	Special Characteristics	Supplier

Trees

Variety	Description	Date Planted	Location	Number Planted	Special Characteristics	Supplier

Trees

Variety	Description	Date Planted	Location	Number Planted	Special Characteristics	Supplier

Love–letters in Flowers

An exquisite invention this,
Worthy of Love's most honeyed kiss,
This art of writing billet-doux
In buds, and odours, and bright hues!

—Leigh Hunt

POTPOURRI

Potpourri

Someday, your children (and grandchildren) will appreciate your efforts in keeping these notes and records, especially if they complete the pages set aside for the children's garden. Here, they can keep simple records, draw and label their garden layout, or insert a photo of their personal efforts. Please encourage them to do so. Also included are pages for your own garden photos. A yearly photograph of a favorite garden spot can show how much change takes place over a span of five years—due of course, to your very hard work!

I have tried to include a wide variety of gardening topics that a majority of gardeners would find useful, but there are several untitled charts near the end of the journal for those who have other areas of interest. You might use these for recording any number of activities, such as the following examples.

- egg production
- grain crop production
- maple syrup production
- roadside sales
- cordwood chopped and burned each year
- goat milk production
- small animal breeding (goats, rabbits)
- favorite garden recipes
- the culturing of orchids
- the Japanese art of bonsai
- a list of visitors to your garden
- garden finances
- birds

"Tickle it with a hoe and it will laugh into a harvest

— Douglas Jerrold

Firsts & Lasts

Farming lore has it that corn can be planted when the leaves of an elm tree are the size of squirrels' ears. Father used to say beans could be planted when one could comfortably sit, bare-bottom, in the garden soil; if your bottom felt warm after one minute it was time to plant!

There are countless examples of rural pioneers making such observations and acting accordingly. Likewise, the present-day gardener can, by observing and recording the dates of various garden events, make a rather simple but effective comparative check on a whole host of garden happenings, particularly in terms of weather conditions. Checking back through previous years reveals patterns in budding, flowering and leafing dates. Knowledge of annual events in the natural world allows the gardener to determine other activities, such as the time particular seedlings may be transplanted into the garden. In other words, does the bite from the first black fly indicate that it's time to plant peas?

I am not suggesting that all records must be designed to predict the weather or the outbreak of insect invasions. Just as a matter of curiosity, I find it interesting to know when the garden was turned over each spring and fall, or when the thieving squirrels began to steal our hazelnuts. This chart can record scientific observations, predictions, superstitions, the simplest of mundane gardening events, or any combination thereof.

Here are some activities you might wish to include in your own list.

- The first and last rose of the season.
- The arrival and departure date of a particular bird or insect.
- The first berry, fruit, flower or vegetable of the season
- Particular garden maintenance jobs.
- The first and last feeding of pond fish.
- The first and last frost of the year.

In the hope of reaching the moon,
men fail to see the flowers that blossom at their feet.

–Albert Schweitzer

Firsts & Lasts of the Season

Observation, Event, Task	Year		Year		Year		Year		Year	
	First	Last	First	Last	First	Last	First	Last	First	Last

Firsts & Lasts of the Season

Observation, Event, Task	Year		Year		Year		Year		Year	
	First	Last	First	Last	First	Last	First	Last	First	Last

Harvesting

Even though I was only eight at the time, I can clearly recall many of the details of October 4, 1952. Our family was returning from Sunday morning church in Osnabruck Centre, Stormont County, in the lower Ottawa Valley. As we turned onto the 5th concession where our 115-acre farm was located, we spotted a huge billow of smoke rising above the trees in the vicinity of our modest farm. Mother, tears already in her eyes, said, "I hope it's the barn." Without a moment's hesitation, Father countered, "I hope it's the house." He got his wish. I guess he had instantaneously calculated that his family could still be provided for if our milk cows, chickens and pigs were still alive; Mother, in her own instant of grief, wished for the necessities and comforts of home, humble as it was.

The following day, Father partially recanted; the day before our farmhouse burned to the ground, he had dumped his entire crop of freshly dug potatoes into the root cellar. The onions, beets, carrots and apples were also stored down there,

along with Mother's fruit preserves, jams, jellies and pickles. The entire harvest, our winter's supply of food, had literally gone up in smoke. (Ironically, about a year later, our cattle were struck with foot-and-mouth disease, effectively putting an end to our farming days—but that's a whole other story.)

Root cellars still exist in those old rural farmhouses, and if you are fortunate enough to have one, I hope you put it to good use. Most newer homes do not contain the luxury of a root cellar (builders, please note), but it's often possible to convert part of a basement or room for fruit and vegetable storage.

Ventilation, temperature and humidity will be your three main concerns. Vegetables such as onions and squash require low humidity, while most root crops store well in moderately moist conditions. Temperature preferences range from near freezing to 15°C (60°F), and it is important to heed both recommended temperatures and humidity requirements in order to maintain crop quality and longevity.

Good ventilation is a must, as many stored fruits and vegetables give off gases. Besides causing unpleasant odors, they reduce vitamin content and cause the ripening process to accelerate, thereby reducing shelf life. An abundance of gardening references contain comprehensive tables, modern-day instructions and time-honored practices for the storage of particular crops (Father used to throw apples in with his potatoes, as the combination prevents the premature sprouting of the latter). Finally, no matter what storage facilities you have, careful digging, picking, plucking and handling is of great importance. If the crops are of excellent quality (no cuts, bruises, decay or disease) when they go into storage, their chances of longevity will be greatly enhanced. Be sure to check them regularly and immediately remove those showing signs of unusual softness or decay.

Use the "Recommended" column in the harvest chart not just to keep track of storage ability, but to indicate whether you would grow it again based on any number of criteria—taste, resistance to pests and disease, size, general quality, yield or even appearance.

In seed time learn, in harvest teach, in winter enjoy.

—William Blake

Harvesting

YEAR _____

Type	Variety	WHEN HARVESTED		YIELD			RECOMMENDED	
		First	Last	Quantity	Quality/Comments	Canned, preserved, frozen, stored, fresh use	Yes	No

Harvesting

YEAR _____

Type	Variety	WHEN HARVESTED		YIELD		Quality/Comments	Canned, preserved, frozen, stored, fresh use	RECOMMENDED	
		First	Last	Quantity				Yes	No

Harvesting

YEAR _____

Type	Variety	WHEN HARVESTED		YIELD			RECOMMENDED	
		First	Last	Quantity	Quality/Comments	Canned, preserved, frozen, stored, fresh use	Yes	No

Harvesting

Type	Variety	WHEN HARVESTED		YIELD			RECOMMENDED	
		First	Last	Quantity	Quality/Comments	Canned, preserved, frozen, stored, fresh use	Yes	No

Harvesting

YEAR _____

| Type | Variety | WHEN HARVESTED | | YIELD | | | RECOMMENDED | |
		First	Last	Quantity	Quality/Comments	Canned, preserved, frozen, stored, fresh use	Yes	No

Date

Details

Notes on Vegetables

Date

Details

Date

Details

Greenhouse Activities

Date

Details

Notes on Herbs

Details

Date

Notes on Herbs

Details

Date

Lawn Care

Date

Details

Pond Care

Date

Details

Indoor Plants

Date	Details

Indoor Plants

Date	Details

Details

Date

Ne'er-Do-Wells

Date

Details

Container Plantings

Date

Details

Notes on Weather

Details

Date

Notes on Weather

Details

Date

Notes on Weather

Details

Date

Children's Gardens

YEAR

Garden Photo or Illustration

Type	Variety	Date Planted	Date Harvested

Kids, don't forget to water, feed and weed your garden!

Children's Gardens

YEAR

Garden Photo or Illustration

Type	Variety	Date Planted	Date Harvested

Kids, don't forget to water, feed and weed your garden!

Children's Gardens

YEAR

Garden Photo or Illustration

Type	Variety	Date Planted	Date Harvested

Kids, don't forget to water, feed and weed your garden!

117

Children's Gardens

YEAR

Garden Photo or Illustration

Type	Variety	Date Planted	Date Harvested

Children's Gardens

YEAR

Garden Photo or Illustration

Type	Variety	Date Planted	Date Harvested

Kids, don't forget to water, feed and weed your garden!

Subject _____

Year _____

Comments

Garden Photos

Subject

Year

Comments

Garden Photos

Subject _____

Year _____

Comments

Garden Photos

Subject _____

Year _____

Comments

Garden Photos

Subject

Year

Comments

Garden Equipment Purchases

Date

Details

Chart For

Summer Days

In summer, when the days were long,

We walked together in the wood:

Our heart was light, our step was strong;

Sweet flutterings were there in our blood

In summer, when the days are long.

—Anonymous

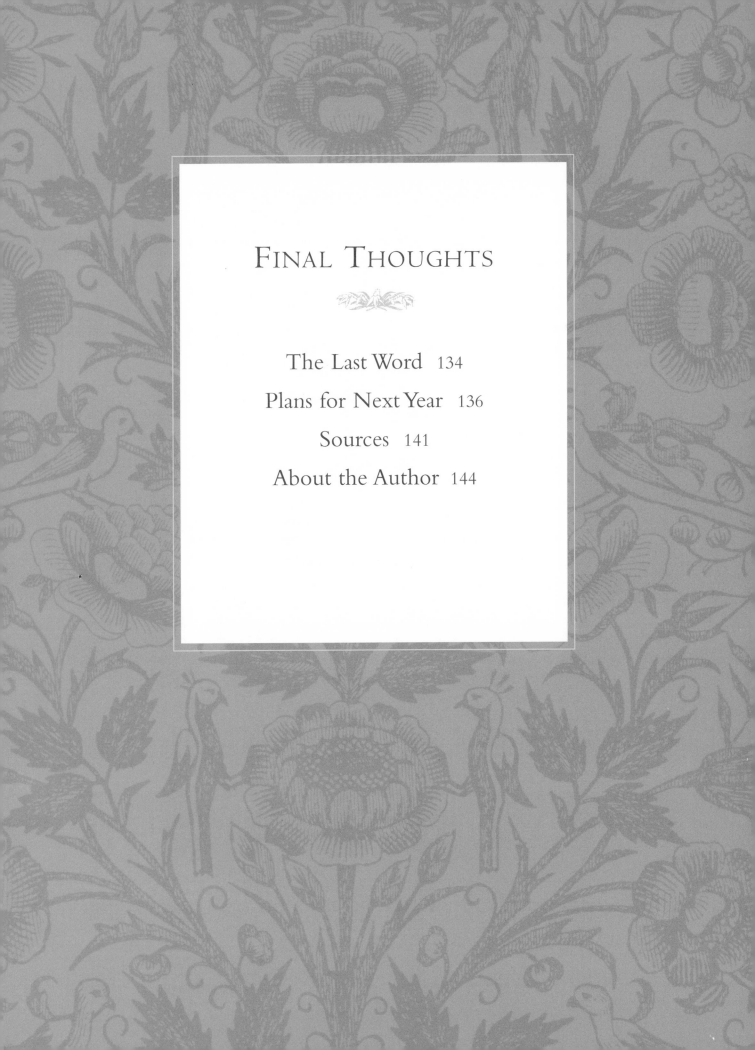

FINAL THOUGHTS

The Last Word

Had it not been for the devastating house fire and crippling outbreak of foot-and-mouth disease, we would probably not have sold the farm and moved to Ottawa. Leaving familiar surroundings was not easy. I pined—and still do—for haylofts, open fields, creeks, winter sleigh rides, the local blacksmith shop, and Father's machinery, especially his Massey-Harris tractor. Regretfully, my parents did not keep journals of our days on the 5th concession of Osnabruck Township, but I do have a good collection of farm photos (fortunately saved from the fire) through which I can browse.

This final set of charts is for planning your garden and outdoor requirements for the next five years. Here you can jot down plans, ideas and products as they cross your mind throughout the course of the year. They might include a note about a new approach to some aspect of the garden, notation of a particular variety of plant or seed you would like to try next year, or simply a brief reminder to purchase a new soaker hose when they come on sale next spring. For easy access, these pages are near the end of the journal, as I suspect they will be frequently used. The very last pages are for recording sources of information. These might include radio and television programs, newspapers, magazines, Web sites, gardening books and local gardening experts.

Before I close, I would like to include one final paragraph to vent a personal frustration that equals insect invasion, blight, drought and untimely frost. Sometimes it seems I spend most of my gardening time trying to convert grams, ounces, teaspoons, tablespoons, square metres, kilograms, and all other weights and measures into the required mixture as instructed on the various garden product containers. A calculator has become an integral part of my gardening equipment and is kept close by at all times. I have, therefore, one request of the gardening industry: you make wonderful products, but please, make it simple for us gardeners. We would be most grateful if you were to talk to us in terms of a handful, cupful, or pinch per plant rather than grams per litre of water for each 100 square metres of garden! It would be so much easier. If it is possible, we thank you.

I have written quite enough. I wish each of you the very best in your gardening ventures, and I hope this journal will help you remember all that is needed for growing greener greens and reaping the benefits and pleasures of gardening.

Now, if you will excuse me, I must go down to the garden to do some serious hoeing.

Show me your garden and I shall tell you what you are.

—Alfred Austin

Details

Date

Plans for Next Year

Date

Details

Plans for Next Year

Date

Details

Plans for Next Year

Date	Details

Plans for Next Year

Date

Details

Sources

Topic

Source and Information

141

Sources

Topic

Source and Information